C000245247

The
Unitarians

by
Jeremy and
Rosemary Goring

FOREWORD BY
REVD ARTHUR LONG, M.A.
PRINCIPAL, UNITARIAN COLLEGE, MANCHESTER

RELIGIOUS AND MORAL EDUCATION PRESS
An Imprint of Arnold-Wheaton

Religious and Moral Education Press
An Imprint of Arnold-Wheaton
Hennock Road, Exeter EX2 8RP

Pergamon Press Ltd
Headington Hill Hall, Oxford OX3 0BW

Pergamon Press Inc.
Maxwell House, Fairview Park, Elmsford,
New York 10523

Pergamon Press Canada Ltd
Suite 104, 150 Consumers Road, Willowdale,
Ontario M2J 1P9

Pergamon Press (Australia) Pty Ltd
P.O. Box 544, Potts Point, N.S.W. 2011

Pergamon Press GmbH
Hammerweg 6, D-6242 Kronberg,
Federal Republic of Germany

First edition 1984

Printed in Great Britain by A Wheaton & Co. Ltd, Exeter
ISBN 0 08-030606-3 non net
ISBN 0 08-030607-1 net

Contents

ACKNOWLEDGEMENTS

Thanks are due to the following for permission to reproduce photographs: the Trustees of Dr Williams's Library, London (page 20), Arthur Hamer (page 36, top), John Hewerdine (pages 33, 47, 49), International Association for Religious Freedom (page 55), Nancy Richards (page 24, 31).

COVER PHOTOGRAPH: *The Reverend Penelope Laws outside Dean Row Chapel, Wilmslow, Cheshire (Peter Fletcher Photography)*

Foreword

Unitarians are fond of saying nowadays that theirs is a tradition which is 'outside the mainstream'. To many, they are not only outside the mainstream but quite beyond the pale. In his autobiography, the late L.P. Jacks tells a story of two ecclesiastics at the end of the nineteenth century contemplating with dismay the then newly erected premises of Manchester College, Oxford. 'Even the architecture,' said one, 'is obtrusively Unitarian. Solid and cold – built to last, but not to please. One can imagine it lasting till the Day of Judgment.' 'Ah,' said the other, 'maybe. But it will not last a day longer!'

In their admirable presentation of the history and leading characteristics of the Unitarian movement, Jeremy and Rosemary Goring have dealt clearly and succinctly with a difficult and complex subject. Their informative account underlines the continuing importance of this small denomination which reflects a very radical but a perfectly legitimate aspect of the Protestant tradition, firmly grounded in Christian roots, but rejoicing in an openness to the truths of other faiths, and dedicated to the conviction that 'God fulfils Himself in many ways'.

Arthur J. Long
Principal, Unitarian College, Manchester
President of the Unitarian General Assembly, 1983-4

1

Who Are They?

'Unitarians? Never heard of them!'

In the days when everyone had to do national service, a young man went to join the Army. At the recruiting office he was asked a lot of questions. Age? Parentage? Birthplace? Occupation? And finally, Religion? 'Unitarian,' he said. The recruiting officer was quite taken aback. 'Oh!' he exclaimed. 'Is that official?'

Many people have never heard of them, it is true, but in fact the Unitarians are one of the oldest nonconformist denominations in Britain. They have made a significant contribution to the country's religious life and, like the Quakers, they have played an important part in movements for social, economic and political reform. Even today, when churches are generally less active than they were in the past, Unitarians still exercise an influence out of all proportion to their numbers.

Why, then, have so few people heard of them? One reason is that, compared with other nonconformist groups, there are not many of them. No one knows exactly how many there are, since there has never been a census, but the total number in the British Isles is probably only about 15 000, the equivalent of the crowd at a second-division football match. There are only about 250 congregations and these are not spread evenly over the country. For example, Unitarian congregations are thick on the ground in Greater Manchester, Merseyside and parts of South Wales, thin on the ground in Essex and Northamptonshire, and completely non-existent in Herefordshire and Cornwall. This means that awareness of the existence of Unitarians is greater in some places than in others: they may be unknown in Liskeard but very well known in Liverpool.

Another reason why Unitarians are comparatively unknown is that they are, on the whole, reluctant to publicise themselves. Some of them are even unwilling to advertise the Unitarian name, preferring to call themselves 'Free Christian'. On some church notice-boards the name appears, if at all, in very small type underneath 'The Old Meeting House', 'Green Street Chapel' or some other neutral-sounding title. For the general public, it is as confusing as if different branches of a supermarket chain were to trade under different names in different towns.

The Unitarian symbol of the flaming chalice, representing the flame of living truth within the cup of shared faith.

This tendency to keep a low profile is not entirely accidental. It stems from a deep-rooted dislike of intolerant attitudes, and a positive unwillingness to thrust their beliefs down other people's throats. This, they feel, would go against their deeply felt principles of Freedom, Reason and Tolerance. It also has something to do with their history. Like all the older nonconformist denominations, they are the successors of people who, many years ago, were actively persecuted for their beliefs. They had to hold their services of worship in secret for fear that the authorities would find them and punish them by fines or imprisonment, and so they became accustomed to keeping their heads down. Even after the penal laws had been repealed Unitarians, unlike other nonconformists, continued to experience persecution of a subtler kind. Because their beliefs conflicted with those of most other church people they were often regarded with great hostility. This attitude persists even today. Not so long ago a group of young people were discussing religion with an Anglican vicar when someone happened to mention the Unitarians. 'Oh!' he said. 'Don't have anything to do with *them*. They're not Christians.'

So here is another reason why so few people have ever heard of the Unitarians: some of those who do know about them do not like to talk about them.

2

What's Different about Them?

'They're not Christians: they don't believe in Jesus.'

On Sunday, 22 October 1933 the Reverend Lawrence Redfern, a Unitarian minister, preached in Liverpool Cathedral at the invitation of the Dean. He was a gifted preacher and his sermon was, by all accounts, eloquent, moving and not at all controversial. But some people – who had not themselves been present at the service – said it was a 'grave scandal' against the Church of England, and consequently the Convocation of York decided that no Unitarian ought ever again to be allowed to preach in an Anglican church.

What is the reason for this prejudice against Unitarians? It is mainly because of their name. A Unitarian, according to the dictionary, is someone who 'denies the doctrine of the Trinity'. Many people have therefore got the idea that the Unitarians' main purpose in life is to attack the Trinity. However, Unitarians do not spend their time attacking other people's beliefs. They have positive beliefs of their own. Contrary to what is sometimes said, most of them do 'believe in Jesus', but they see him as a man to be followed rather than as God to be worshipped. 'Why do you keep calling me Lord, Lord, and never do what I tell you?' is a text which they take seriously. Rather than ooking on Jesus as 'the only begotten Son of God' they regard him as one who came to enable all people to realise their true nature as God's children.

Although Unitarians do not attack traditional doctrines, they do insist that no doctrine is too sacred to be questioned. If men make doctrines, men – and women – must also be free to unmake them. Since the mid nineteenth century, when they gradually abandoned their belief in an infallible Bible, Unitarians have maintained that no written words – not even the words written in the New Testament – are too sacred to be questioned.

It is perhaps this questioning, 'scientific' attitude to religious truth that most sets Unitarians apart. Joseph Priestley, one of the founding fathers of the denomination, was also one of the greatest scientists of his day. Since his time the Unitarian outlook has continued to have a special appeal for those who wish to explore the relationship between the truths of religion and truth as discovered in the laboratory. Indeed, Sir Alister Hardy, F.R.S., the distinguished zoologist who is also a prominent Unitarian layman, has recently set up a special Research Unit at Manchester College, Oxford, in which religious experience can be subjected to scientific analysis.

With the scientific attitude goes a marked independence of mind. Unitarians, like Quakers, will not join the World Council of Churches because they cannot accept the formula 'Christ as God'. Like the Quakers, they have no fixed creeds. They believe that people must be free to 'work out their own salvation', to formulate their own beliefs in the light of their own experience. By studying the Bible with an open mind, by reading a variety of books, or simply through serious thought, prayer and discussion with others, they will be able to come to their own first-hand conclusions about the deeper mysteries of life. In answer to the criticism that they 'just believe anything they like', a Unitarian might reply, 'That may be so, but isn't that better than pretending to believe something that you feel, deep down, not to be true?'

However, the practice of religion can never be a purely 'do-it-yourself' affair. There will always be the need for a church or fellowship in which people can meet together to share their experiences. Unitarians believe that in any discussion of religious ideas there must be complete freedom of expression. All ideas, however unusual, 'cranky' or outrageous they may appear to be, have to be tolerated, for who knows through what strange channels the truth will be revealed to our generation?

AGREEING TO DIFFER Thus there is one thing in particular which distinguishes Unitarians from most other religious groups. When it comes to questions of belief, *they agree to differ among themselves*. So, within any one congregation, there can be a great variety of points of view. Some members may be traditional in their outlook, preferring to call themselves 'Free Christians' or 'Liberal Christians'. Their beliefs are not so very different from those held by Unitarians a hundred years ago: they believe in God as a loving Father and revere Jesus as the greatest of his sons. On the other hand there may be others in the congregation who find such language unhelpful. They may prefer to call themselves 'theists' or 'universalists' rather than Christians and to seek inspiration in other books as well as the Bible. And there may also be some who, feeling that the word 'God' has little significance, prefer to think simply in terms of Man and his age-old quest for meaning and value. Such people might call themselves 'humanists'. In a Unitarian church all are welcome. People are not excluded on account of the words that come out of their mouths. For Unitarians believe that people's innermost thoughts and feelings are more important than the words they use to describe them.

It will now be clear why Unitarians believe so strongly in Freedom, Reason and Tolerance. They have a high regard for these words and no statement of their beliefs would be complete without them. But there is another word which is perhaps even more important to them: the word 'Conscience'. They believe that Conscience – the 'still small voice' within – is the surest guide to how people should conduct their lives. They believe this strongly, because it was for the sake of conscience that many years ago their forebears broke away from the main body of the Church and set up their own free Christian congregations.

Think about . . .

s it ever right for a church to exclude a preacher from its
ulpit? Should there be any limits to freedom of speech in
church?

What do you understand by religious truth and truth as
evealed by science? Are there any differences between
hem?

Is it a good thing or not for people to have to work out
heir beliefs for themselves?

3

Early
History

The story of the Unitarians is rather difficult to follow because at first they were not called Unitarians at all. Most often they were called Presbyterians.

THE ENGLISH PRESBYTERIANS   The Presbyterians were a group of Puritans who, in company with the Independents, were turned out of the Church of England in 1662. How this came about has been well described in Jan Baker's book in this series, *The Church of England*: 'In 1662 the new Prayer Book was approved, and another Act of Uniformity required that everyone take an oath agreeing to use the book. Many Puritans asked for alterations which would allow them to continue in the Church with a good conscience, but their requests were not granted. As a result almost 2000 ministers left the Church of England.' These ministers and the people who followed them became known as nonconformists or dissenters. The Presbyterians were very different from their namesakes in Scotland, who had set up a Calvinistic form of church government, complete with 'presbyteries' and 'synods'. The English Presbyterians were not interested in such things: they had more in common with the Independents or Congregationalists, who had been forced to leave the Church of England at the same time.

The pulpit (built in 1621) in Kidderminster Unitarian Church from which Richard Baxter preached in 1785

There was, however, an important difference between the Independents and the Presbyterians. The Independents believed in a 'gathered Church' or closed community of Christ's elect, to which people could be admitted only if they could prove that they were 'saved'. The Presbyterians, on the other hand, believed in the Church Universal, to which all Christians belonged unless they had deliberately excluded themselves. They were reluctant nonconformists. They were followers of Richard Baxter, who dreamed of reunion with a truly catholic (i.e. universal) national Church, broadminded enough to include all Christians.

By the early eighteenth century the gulf between the Presbyterians and the Independents was growing wider. While the Independents remained Calvinist in doctrine (believing that Christ had died for a specially selected few) the Presbyterians became Arminian (believing, with the Dutch theologian Arminius, that he had died for the sake of everyone). But what most distinguished the Presbyterians was their *attitude* to doctrines. They did not like to see man-made doctrines being used as a test of faith. Matters came to a head in 1719 when a meeting was held at Salters' Hall in London to decide whether doctrinal tests should be imposed upon students for the ministry; most of the Independents were in favour of tests; all but a handful of Presbyterians were against.

CHANGES IN DOCTRINE While moving away from the Independents the Presbyterians were drawing closer to the Anglicans, who at this time were generally more radical in outlook than the nonconformists. Some Anglicans were even saying that the Christianity found in the Scriptures was different from that found in the creeds. Under their influence John Taylor, Presbyterian minister at Norwich, wrote a book called *The Scripture Doctrine of Original Sin* (1740). He concluded that the Bible did not support the idea that human nature was fundamentally bad. The book had a devastating influence. As one hostile critic put it, 'It is a bad book and a dangerous book and an heretical book; and what is worse than all, the book is unanswerable.'

When they studied the Bible the Presbyterians had two main aims. One was to reconcile Christian faith with the new scientific outlook of the times. The other was to get back to 'the religion of Christ in its

16

riginal simplicity and native beauty, free from adulteration and mixture'. When their opponents called them 'new-scheme preachers', hey retorted that their scheme was 'as old as the Apostles'.

The Presbyterian leaders may have been able scholars and good pastors but their preaching, apparently, was not always very exciting. The average sermon, with its carefully reasoned arguments and high moral tone, appealed more to the head than to the heart. It is not surprising, then, that some of the humbler, less intellectual hearers vent off to listen to the fiery gospel preachers (known as evangelicals) who, inspired by the examples of Wesley and Whitfield, were then preaching to the poor and downtrodden. Indeed, it was partly because of the withdrawal of such people that the Presbyterian congregations were so much smaller in the second half of the eighteenth century than they had been earlier. With the tide running strongly in favour of the evangelicals, the outlook for the rational dissenters (those who preferred reasoned argument) looked bleak. They had fine wares to offer, but no one seemed to want to buy. They lacked any sense of direction and, as a denomination, they seemed in danger of disintegrating.

But as old doors were shutting, new ones were opening. Soon the denomination was to have new leadership, a new identity and a new name.

Think about . . .

Visit an old parish church and look at the list of rectors or vicars to see whether a new one was appointed in 1662. If so, the man before him was probably ejected. If your local library has a copy of *Calamy Revised*, by A. G. Matthews, you can look up the minister's name and find out more about him.

Read Chapter 2 of Kenneth Slack's *The United Reformed Church* in this series. How did the early Presbyterians differ from the Independents? How did the old English Presbyterians differ from those who are now part of the United Reformed Church?

Many people see Richard Baxter as a pioneer of the ecumenical movement (the movement towards unity in the Christian Churches). Read his biography and find out why.

4

A New Identity

THEOPHILUS LINDSEY   In 1763 a new vicar arrived in the north Yorkshire parish of Catterick. His name was Theophilus Lindsey and he was then forty years old. He set about his parish duties with such unusual enthusiasm that people called him a 'Methodist'. (The group of people known as Methodists, at that time still within the Church of England, were noted for their enthusiastic preaching.) He was a devoted pastor and he gave away much of his money to the poor.

However, his conscience troubled him: he could not agree with all the teachings of his Church. Like many other Anglicans at this time, he found that he could no longer accept the doctrine of the Trinity, and so he began to call himself a 'Unitarian'. In 1773 he resigned his vicarage and he and his wife moved to London. Although Lindsey had few possessions he had many good friends, with whose help he rented an auction-room in Essex Street off the Strand and turned it into a chapel. He made it known that the chapel was to be for Unitarian worship – a risky thing to do at that date. Until the passing of the Unitarian Relief Act in 1813 it was a criminal offence to deny the doctrine of the Trinity. This was the first openly Unitarian place of worship in the British Isles.

JOSEPH PRIESTLEY   At the opening service in the chapel on 17 Apr
1774 about 200 people were present. Among them was a youn
Presbyterian minister called Joseph Priestley, who had recently com
to London from Leeds. He was a brilliant scientist and was soon t
become famous as the discoverer of oxygen. He brought the sam
scientific spirit to the study of the Bible and Church History and h
became one of the most controversial religious writers of his day. A
this time he was working on a book called *History of the Corruptions o
Christianity*. He believed that the doctrine of the Trinity was part o

Joseph Priestley (an engraving of a portrait by Fuseli)

e 'corruption' and, like Lindsey, he called himself a Unitarian. However, Priestley had been brought up as an Independent and his outlook was sectarian, i.e. he believed in the division of people into groups according to their beliefs about religious doctrines. He wanted to create a new Unitarian sect partly inside and partly outside the old loose federation of Presbyterian congregations.

Not many Presbyterians welcomed this new development. They disliked the 'Unitarian' label because it caused controversy and cut them off from other Christians. They preferred to stick to the catholic ideals of John Taylor, who had insisted that 'we are Christians and only Christians and disown all connection, excepting that of love and goodwill, with any sect or party whatever'. Nor were many Presbyterians in sympathy with the radical political ideas that led Priestley and his friends to welcome American Independence and the French Revolution. Priestley's republican enthusiasm earned him the name of 'Gunpowder Joe', and so strong was the feeling against him that in 1791 a patriotic mob burned down the New Meeting House in Birmingham (where he had ministered since 1780) and also his house and those of other prominent Unitarians in the town. Three years later he emigrated to America.

NEW BEGINNINGS   Soon after Priestley's departure, the Presbyterian/ Unitarian denomination was greatly strengthened by the addition of many congregations of General Baptists. As the descendants of the fifteenth-century heretics known as Lollards, these Baptists could claim to be the oldest nonconformist sect in the kingdom. They had a liberal attitude to doctrine and at the end of the eighteenth-century many of them declared themselves to be Unitarians. But they differed from the Presbyterians/Unitarians in a number of ways. For one thing they were more sectarian and less outward looking. They were also less 'respectable' socially: while the Presbyterians were mainly middle class the Baptists were generally people of humbler origin. They were less well educated, less intellectual, less suspicious of 'enthusiasm'. Some of them became ardent promoters of their faith and were among the most active supporters of the Unitarian Fund set up in 1806 to finance new developments. Richard Wright, son of a Norfolk farm labourer, became the Fund's first travelling missionary, trudging on

Ditchling Unitarian Chapel, a typical meeting-house first occupied by the General Baptists

foot through the length of England, often preaching his simple gospel in barns or in the open air.

Wright was largely responsible for bringing into the Unitarian fold a group of independent Methodist congregations in east Lancashire known as the 'Cookites'. They were so named after Joseph Cooke, a minister at Rochdale, who in 1806 was expelled by the Methodist Conference for heresy. At the time of his death in 1811 at the early age of thirty-five, his followers numbered more than 1000, grouped around sixteen preaching-stations and served by eighteen local preachers and prayer-leaders. Like the General Baptists the Cookites were mostly poor people and their attachment to the Unitarians was a further step in broadening the denomination's social base. They also contributed some much-needed Methodist enthusiasm.

Wright's travels also took him into Scotland and Wales. In South Wales ministers trained at the Presbyterian Academy in Carmarthen had long had a liberalizing influence on nonconformity, especially in the towns and villages of the Teifi valley in Cardiganshire. The most influential of these was David Davis, minister at Llwynrhydowen

rom 1773 until his death in 1827. He was a celebrated poet and
classical scholar: his school at Castle Howell Farm was attended by
boys from all over Wales and was known as the 'Athens of
Cardiganshire'. Although he himself would not use any
denominational label, he was in fact the principal founding father of
the Unitarian movement in this part of Wales, so famous for its
radicalism that it became known as the 'Black Spot'.

Denominational activities in England and Wales were co-ordinated
by the British and Foreign Unitarian Association, a body established
in 1825. The success of its propaganda alarmed some of the other
nonconformists, who denounced the Unitarians as heretics. As a
result, in 1837 the Presbyterian/Unitarian members were forced to
withdraw from the General Body of Protestant Ministers which, for
over a century, had represented the joint interests of the old
established nonconformist groups in and around London.

JAMES MARTINEAU   These developments also worried some of the
more traditional English Presbyterians, who objected to the use of
'Unitarian'as a denominational label. Foremost among these objectors
was James Martineau. Born in 1805 into an old Presbyterian family of
Huguenot descent, he had been brought up at the Octagon Chapel in
Norwich, where John Taylor had formerly ministered. After a long
ministry in Liverpool Martineau moved to London in 1857 to become
tutor (and later principal) at Manchester College, the major centre of
training for Unitarian ministers at that time. He became more and
more out of sympathy with the militant Unitarianism of his day,
which he found 'critical, cold and untrusting', and pleaded for a
warmer, more emotional kind of religion. His writings earned him the
respect and admiration of Christians of all denominations. A. M.
Fairbairn, a leading Congregationalist, said of him: 'In the whole
nineteenth century there lived no man of subtler thought, of more
exquisite imagination, of finer character, of purer spirit.'

Martineau was ecumenical in outlook and planned an inter-
denominational 'Free Christian Union'. To counter the influence of
the British and Foreign Unitarian Association he formed a 'National
Conference of Unitarian, Liberal Christian, Free Christian,
Presbyterian and other Non-Subscribing or Kindred Congregations'

The building that housed Manchester New College when James Martineau was principal. It is now occupied by Dr Williams's Library

– a triumph, one might say, of Victorian verbosity. But the length of the name reflected the breadth of Martineau's vision: he longed to see a broad, all-inclusive national Church in which Christians of every kind could feel at home. So, from now on, the denomination (in the words of the historian, H.L. Short) 'seemed to consist of two overlapping circles, one labelled "Unitarian" and eager for organisation and propaganda, the other rejecting labels and treasuring comprehensiveness.' Each side had its own college, its own newspaper and its own hymn-book, but the two 'circles' did overlap. Faced with a choice between two sorts of institution, many Unitarians cheerfully patronised both.

The splitting in two of such a small denomination naturally resulted in a certain waste of resources and so, as the twentieth century progressed, strenuous efforts were made to heal the breach. Finally, in 1928, the National Conference and the British and Foreign Unitarian Association were merged into the newly formed General

Assembly of Unitarian and Free Christian Churches. Today 'Unitarians' and 'Free Christians' may not always see eye to eye, but this does not worry them very much. As successors of those who were ejected in 1662, their prime concern has always been unity, not uniformity.

THE DEVOPMENT OF UNITARIANISM IN RELATION TO OTHER DENOMINATIONS

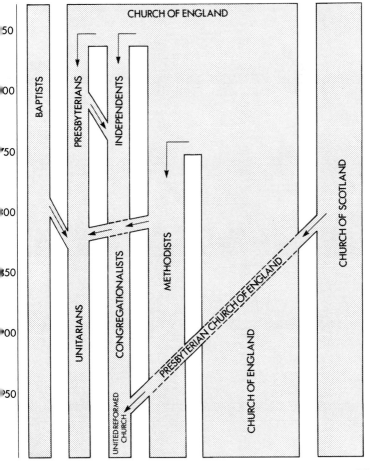

Think about . . .

Joseph Priestley is the only figure in the *Dictionary of National Biography* whose career is described in two instalments by two different experts. Read the entries in the *Dictionary* to find out why.

Look up the word 'Unitarian' in as many dictionaries, encyclopaedias and other reference books as you can. Do the definitions differ?

If there is a Unitarian church in your neighbourhood, find out all you can about its history.

5

Practical Work and Service

Although, throughout their history, Unitarians have differed from other denominations in some of their ideas and ways of thinking, they have shared a common Christian conviction that actions are more important than words. In view of their small numbers their record of practical work and service is worth some consideration.

It was this record that the Dean of Liverpool had in mind when in 1933 he described the exclusion of the Unitarians from Anglican pulpits as 'a sin against truth and an outrage upon God'. He spoke admiringly of the Unitarian contribution to the enrichment of Liverpool's civic life. He recalled the devotion of John Johns, first minister of the city's Domestic Mission, founder of the Liverpool Ragged School and of the Mechanics' Institute, and hero of the Irish famine of 1846, who 'lived in the spirit of his great office and died its sacrifice'. He also praised the dedication of three Unitarian laypeople: William Roscoe, 'Christian philanthropist, leader against the Slave Trade, first president and chief founder of Liverpool's Royal Institute'; Catherine Wilkinson, 'greatest of workers among the poor, whose memory is honoured in our cathedral in the window where her portrait is set among famous women'; William Rathbone, 'founder of the District Nursing Association and, more than any other man, of our University, whom Florence Nightingale called "one of God's best sons"'. 'These,' the Dean of Liverpool wrote, 'are a few out of the very many whom Unitarianism has inspired to Christian service.'

CITIES AND TOWNS Similar instances of 'Christian service' can be found in Bristol, another city with a strong Unitarian presence. Here the greatest influence was Martineau's old teacher, Lant Carpenter, minister of Lewin's Mead Meeting from 1817 to 1839. He took a leading part in public causes, always in close co-operation with other denominations. His biographer tells how on one occasion when a list of committee members was being drawn up for a newly founded philanthropic society, 'a clergyman rose and said that he must consider any list incomplete which did not contain the respected name of Dr Carpenter'. His very practical Christian concern was inherited by his daughter Mary, who devoted her life to the care of poor children in Bristol. On her own initiative she created a day school for the neglected, an industrial school for the homeless and a reformatory school for those convicted in the courts. After her death in 1877 the Dean of Bristol arranged for a monument to be set up in her memory in the cathedral. On it are the words: 'No human ill escaped her pity or cast down her trust. With true self-sacrifice she followed in the train of Christ, to seek and to save that which was lost.' But she could not have done all this without the backing of Unitarians who were active in the civic life of Bristol.

There were several other cities in which Unitarians were equally prominent at this time. In Birmingham Dr H. W. Crosskey, minister of the 'Church of the Messiah' (Priestley's 'New Meeting' in a new guise), made the call for 'Christian citizenship' the keynote of his preaching. It was he who inspired Joseph Chamberlain, a member of the church and mayor of the city from 1873 to 1876, to carry through a great programme of reform: Chamberlain provided the inhabitants with cheap gas, pure water, healthier houses and better schools, and for a time Birmingham was known as 'the best governed city in the world'. In Leeds much improvement work was carried out by a distinguished succession of Unitarian mayors, four of whom were knighted for their services. In Leicester the first five mayors elected after the town government was reformed in 1835 were members of the Unitarian Great Meeting, which came to be known as the 'Mayors' Nest'. Members of the congregation continued to play a leading part in the town's corporate life: it was largely due to their imaginative approach to town planning and public health that Leicester became 'the cleanest industrial town in England'.

In terms of social service the most remarkable Unitarian innovation was the 'Domestic Mission'. The first was founded in London in 1835 and later ones were established in Manchester, Liverpool, Leeds and elsewhere. Unlike the Foreign Missions then being established by other religious bodies, the Domestic Missions were not designed to convert people to anything. The missioner was expected 'to apply his faith rather than to preach it'. His job was a practical one: to help the poor to help themselves. He was to visit them in their homes and offer them friendship, help and advice. He provided them with the means of self-improvement: penny banks, clothing clubs, reading-rooms, Sunday schools and week-night classes in 'the three Rs'. In due course services of worship were added, but this was almost always in response to popular demand. The Missions met a real need, but by the middle years of this century, with the coming of the Welfare State, they were largely redundant. The last to survive was the Liverpool Mission, which in 1974 was amalgamated with the Florence Institute in Toxteth, one of the largest youth welfare agencies in Britain.

INDUSTRY Unitarian reforming zeal was not confined to large towns and cities. It also characterised the activities of industrialists in the countryside. Unitarian manufacturers often had an unusually enlightened attitude to industrial relations. When in the late eighteenth century the Strutt family built their new cotton mills at Belper in Derbyshire they provided schools, a library, a dance-hall and a swimming-bath (complete with instructor) for their workforce. When their contemporaries, the Gregs, built a cotton factory at Styal near Wilmslow in Cheshire, they put up a well-appointed 'apprentice house' where 100 poor children were well cared for by members of the Greg family. Again, the Fieldens of Todmorden (now in West Yorkshire) were cotton masters with a conscience: in 1846 John

Erected by friends as a memorial
of their esteem and respect for

John Pounds

who, while earning his livelihood
by mending shoes, gratuitously
educated and partly clothed and fed
some hundreds of poor children.

HE DIED SUDDENLY ON THE FIRST of JANUARY 1839
AGED 72 YEARS.

" Thou shalt be blessed; for ....
.... they cannot recompense thee."

This memorial is in the John Pounds Memorial Church, Portsmouth

Fielden, M.P. was the man largely responsible for the Act that reduced the hours worked by factory children. The Fieldens also built a factory school for their young employees in which some of the teaching was done by the local Unitarian minister.

EDUCATION   Education has always been a major Unitarian concern. Long before there was a national system of education many congregations established non-denominational day-schools for the children of their neighbourhoods. Unitarians were also pioneers of 'ragged schools' for the children of the very poor. The first such school was founded in Portsmouth in 1818 by John Pounds, a crippled shoemaker, to whose memory the recently rebuilt Unitarian church there has been dedicated. For the adult poor who wished to acquire a basic education there were 'Mechanics' Institutes', the first of which was opened by Unitarians in Nottingham in 1798 and the second in Bristol in 1814.

At the other end of the scale Unitarians played an important part in the provision of higher education. In the eighteenth century,

Manchester College Oxford, still a major Unitarian training centre

31

prevented from entering Oxford and Cambridge, their Presbyteria ancestors had set up a number of Dissenting Academies. One of them Warrington (1757–86), had offered tuition in history, moder languages, chemistry and a wide range of subjects rarely taugh elsewhere: it has been called 'the first red-brick university'. In th nineteenth century Unitarians played a prominent part in foundin University College, London, the 'godless institution in Gower Stree whose creation stimulated the Anglicans to found King's College i the Strand. Unitarians were also among the chief founders of th universities of Manchester, Liverpool, Birmingham and Sheffield.

In the twentieth century Unitarians have continued to take a kee interest in education. A high proportion of them are teachers i schools, colleges and universities. One ex-teacher, James Chuter Ede M.P., later a distinguished President of the General Assembly c Unitarian and Free Christian Churches, was one of the chief architec of the 1944 Education Act. In recent years the Hibbert Trust, Unitarian fund founded in 1847 by Robert Hibbert for 'the spread o Christianity in its simplest and most intelligible form', has sponsore a number of unusual educational ventures, including a series o religious 'Any Questions?' sessions for schoolchildren.

RECENT VENTURES   During the Second World War the same Trus extended its activities into the field of social service. Concerned abou the welfare of British forces overseas, it established a series of 'Hibber Houses' in the Middle and Near East. They were run by a Unitaria minister and a staff of lay assistants who provided hoste accommodation, clubs, bookshops and mobile canteens. Betwee 1941 and 1966 there were in all over twenty centres, most of them wit chapels and 'quiet rooms'. The last overseas hostel was in Cyprus: i was closed in 1966 after the reduction of the island's garrison. Th Trust now runs a hostel for young people in north London.

The latest Unitarian venture in the social service field is the 'Send-a child-to-Hucklow Fund' set up in 1962 by two young ministers from the Manchester district. Great Hucklow is a small village in the Peak District of Derbyshire where a Unitarian Holiday Centre has lon been situated. In the past it was used mainly by Unitarian Sunday schools from the North of England, but now it is used more by

Some children attending one of the special holidays organised by the Send-a-child-to-Hucklow Fund

children from outside the denomination who are sent there by the fund. They come from deprived areas, such as Toxteth in Liverpool, and normally parties of twenty-five spend a week at Hucklow, where they are looked after by the Fund's voluntary helpers. Each year up to 250 children stay at Hucklow. The scheme has caught the imagination of the Unitarian movement and most congregations contribute to it.

This is a good example of the practical Unitarian approach to things. But, as a survey carried out in 1980 made clear, Unitarians do not see their churches primarily as social service agencies. When asked what part of the life of the local church they considered the most important, only a fraction answered, 'Service to the community'. The overwhelming majority replied, 'Worship'.

Think about . . .

Read Chapter 4 of *The Society of Friends* in this series. What have the Unitarians and the Quakers in common?

Find out all you can about the life and work of Mary Carpenter. (The book *Mary Carpenter and the Children of the Streets*, by J. Manton may be available in your local library.)

Find out what social improvements have been made in your town during the last 200 years and what people were responsible for them.

6

Worship

Unitarian churches come in all shapes and sizes. The eighteenth-century ones are usually square boxes, like the big Presbyterian meeting-house in Ipswich or the little General Baptist one in Ditchling, Sussex. But there are a few oddities, such as the eight-sided Octagon Chapel in Norwich, built for John Taylor in 1756 and described by John Wesley as 'perhaps the most elegant meeting-house in Europe'. The nineteenth-century churches are often long, tall and narrow, sometimes with a tower or spire at one end: those at Eccles (in Greater Manchester) and Todmorden look like Anglican parish churches and are frequently mistaken for such. The churches built in this century are generally of more modest proportions, and relatively unpretentious, like the New Meeting in Birmingham, built in 1973 to replace the great gothic 'Church of the Messiah', which was pulled down to make way for a new road scheme.

The forms of worship also vary from place to place. A few congregations use a printed service book called *Orders of Worship* (published in 1932). This contains psalms, litanies and set prayers, some of which are taken from the Anglican Prayer Book of 1662. Unitarians, because of their closer historic ties with the Church of England, have

Unitarian worship centres come in various shapes and sizes, from modest and simple old meeting-houses to ultra-modern churches with attached social centres

Stand Chapel, Whitefield, Greater Manchester

Dean Row, Wilmslow, Cheshire (the church of the minister on the cover)

Bradford Unitarian Church, Yorkshire

Pendleton Unitarian Church and Centre, Manchester

always been more inclined than other nonconformists to use liturgie (i.e. set forms of worship). But today the great majority prefer 'ope services' without prayer books. The commonest form of service what is irreverently called the 'hymn sandwich' – prayers, reading and a sermon, interspersed with hymns. The prayers are generall addressed to God, but some ministers and lay preachers prefer to us meditations which simply involve the hearts and minds of the peopl who are present. Compared with Anglican worship there is mor silence but less 'audience participation'. There are no creeds to recit and usually no responses to say; in an 'open service' the most that th congregation will normally be asked to do, apart from singing hymn: is to join in the Lord's Prayer.

The General Confession is now rarely, if ever, used. This is becaus Unitarians – in church or out of it – do not talk much about 'sins They may admit that everyone is in a state of sin, if this mean separation from God or from 'the highest that they know', but becaus 'sin' is so often associated with a morality based more on fear than o love, they tend to avoid the word altogether. Many would say wit L. P. Jacks (the foremost Unitarian thinker of the twentieth century that Christianity was originally 'a religion of encouragement', i contrast to 'the religion whose keynote is domination, whose metho is repression, whose atmosphere is gloom and whose end is failure The Church, he said, needs to recover 'the lost radiance of th Christian religion' if it is to experience once again the liberating energ of the love of God. Worship, Unitarians believe, is nothing if not 'celebration of life'.

In common with other worshipping communities Unitarian celebrate with hymn-singing. Most congregations use *Hymns c Worship Revised* (1962) – a collection of over 500 hymns drawn from great variety of sources. Many are by Isaac Watts, George Herber Charles Wesley and other great hymn-writers cherished throughou the Christian world. There are also numerous hymns written b Unitarians, both British and American, which are generally less wel known, although some have found their way into collections used b other denominations. (Thirteen are listed on p.42.) However, many o the hymns are more than fifty years old and some people are beginnin to find the language rather dated. A new book, *Hymns for Living*

Inside Plymouth Unitarian Church

39

designed to 'reflect the particular concerns of society in the 1980s', to be published shortly.

Wedged in between the hymns, there are usually two readings in service: originally both would have come from the Bible, but now it common for one to come from another source. It might be an extra from the writings of George Fox, John Bunyan or James Martineau or a poem by Blake, Browning or T. S. Eliot. It might be a passage from some non-Christian source, such as the Hindu Upanishads, the Buddhist Sutras or the Confucianist works of Mencius. Alternatively it might be taken from a very much more up-to-date source, such as an article in the previous day's *Guardian*, a newspaper which was founded and first edited by Unitarians and seems to have a particular place in their affections.

The readings will be closely related to the topic of the sermon which has a place of great importance in Unitarian worship. Sermon vary greatly in style and content. At one extreme is the scholarly essay read at high speed, at the other is the informal 'off-the-cuff' style of delivery, with the 'average' sermon somewhere in between: solid intelligent, logically presented. Sermons usually last about twenty minutes: ministers who go on too long (or, more rarely, not long enough) can come in for congregational criticism. Some minister prefer to lead a discussion in which everyone is encouraged to participate, and sometimes there are 'experimental' services, in which there may be dance, drama, folk music or a candlelight procession. On the whole, however, it is the traditional service which predominates

Besides the Sunday services, there are the occasional services that mark the important milestones in people's lives. Unitarians hold services of baptism – some people call it 'dedication' – when infant are formally received into 'membership of the human family' and the parents dedicate themselves to their care. There is no set form of service: some ministers baptise with water 'in the name of God, our Father, and in the spirit of Jesus Christ'; others take a less traditional line; but all will be guided in some degree by the wishes of the parents The same applies to weddings: the couple will often be invited to help create their own service by choosing not only the hymns but also the prayers and readings. With funerals, too, most ministers will try to adapt the service to individual needs: if, for example, the nearest relative of the dead person is an agnostic for whom traditional religious language has little meaning, the minister will seek to use language which is more suited to the situation.

The only other 'occasional service' held in Unitarian churches is Communion, which is seen primarily as an act of remembrance. Many of the older congregations possess some fine sets of silver Communion plate, but these are not often used. There is a Communion service at the annual meeting of the General Assembly of Unitarian and Free Christian Churches, but few congregations now keep up the old practice of a quarterly celebration. On the whole Unitarians, like Quakers, believe there is more value in inward silence than in outward ceremony.

Some Unitarian fellowships, with no buildings of their own, hold their services in Friends' meeting-houses. Sometimes the two congregations hold joint services, in which the Unitarians appreciate the long Quaker silences and the Quakers enjoy the hymns. Those written by J. G. Whittier, a Quaker with close Unitarian links, are particularly suited to these occasions. One of Whittier's best-known hymns, 'Dear Lord and Father of Mankind', contains the following verse:

> Drop thy still dews of quietness,
> Till all our strivings cease:
> Take from our souls the strain and stress,
> And let our ordered lives confess
> The beauty of thy peace.

A few Unitarian congregations sing this at the end of every service. For many, the words sum up the essence of what they mean by 'worship'.

Well-known hymns written by Unitarians

City of God, how broad and far   (Samuel Johnson)
Come, Kingdom of our God   (John Johns)
Eternal Ruler of the ceaseless round
(John W. Chadwick)
Father, hear the prayer we offer   (Love Maria Willis)
Holy Spirit, Truth Divine   (Samuel Longfellow)
In the Cross of Christ I glory   (Sir John Bowring)
It came upon the midnight clear   (Edmund H. Sears)
Lord of all being, throned afar   (Oliver Wendell Holmes)
Mine eyes have seen the glory of the coming of the
Lord   (Julia Ward Howe)
Nearer, my God, to thee   (Sarah Flower Adams)
Once to every man and nation   (James Russell Lowell)
Though lowly here our lot may be   (William Gaskell)
'Thy Kingdom come!' – on bended knee   (Frederick
Lucian Hosmer)

Think about . . .

Read Chapter 3 of *The Roman Catholic Church* in this series. How does Unitarian worship differ from Catholic worship?

Look at the list of hymns above: you will find most of them in many denominations' hymn-books. Look up the words of any that you do not know. Are there any others by the same authors?

Plan a short service, showing which aspects of worship you consider to be most important.

7

The Importance of Women

In the early years of the nineteenth century there was a Member of Parliament called William Smith who was a prominent Unitarian and a great champion of 'civil and religious liberty'. His part in the abolition of the slave trade was second only to that of his friend William Wilberforce. He was also a strong advocate of Catholic Emancipation. (After the establishment of the Protestant Church in England during the Reformation, Catholics were forbidden to practise their religion or to hold any public position: it was not until the Emancipation Act was passed in 1829 that they regained their civil rights.) However, William Smith is remembered today, if at all, as the grandfather of two remarkable women, both of whom shared his great love of liberty. Both were deeply committed to the cause of women's freedom. One was Barbara Leigh Smith, who in 1855 set up the first Feminist Committee to campaign for women's property rights, and ten years later the first Women's Suffrage Committee. The other was Florence Nightingale.

WOMEN'S RIGHTS   It is not really surprising that these two remarkable women came from Unitarian homes, for here it was usual for girls to be treated more or less on a level with boys. In those days such an attitude was not very common, but Unitarians prided themselves on being reasonable people: to them it seemed most unreasonable to educate their sons and neglect their daughters. Nor did they object too much if their daughters wished to pursue careers that were then considered unsuitable for young ladies.

Because of their emancipated attitudes the Unitarians attracted to their ranks a number of eminent women from more traditional backgrounds. One such was Frances Power Cobbe, an aristocratic Anglo-Irish lady who became the greatest feminist campaigner of the century. After a spell in Bristol, helping Mary Carpenter with her girls' schools, she moved to London and devoted her enormous energies to working for the rights of women. In 1878 she persuaded one of her friends in Parliament to draft a Bill enabling a woman to get a legal separation from a brutal husband. Always the friend of the weak and helpless, she also championed the rights of animals and was founder of the British Union for the Abolition of Vivisection. She wrote several fine hymns and, at a time when most women obeyed St Paul's instruction to 'keep silent in church', she was a frequent preacher in Unitarian pulpits.

WOMEN'S EDUCATION   Some Unitarians, recognising the need for women to have a good education, established schools for girls. As early as 1807 a girls' boarding-school was opened at Gateacre, near Liverpool, by three sisters, Fanny, Harriet and Sarah Lawrence, descendants of Philip Henry, a celebrated ejected minister. They were all devout Unitarians, and most of the 477 girls that they educated in the thirty-year life of the school came from Unitarian homes. They set an example which was later to be consciously followed by their three great-nieces, Penelope, Dorothy and Millicent Lawrence, who opened a small girls' boarding-school in Brighton in 1885. Although the school was officially non-denominational, most of the first pupils came from the same denomination as the founders. The early school registers read like a roll-call of the names of leading Unitarian families: Scott, Courtauld, Nettlefold, Brunner, Martineau. The school prospered and in 1899 it moved to an imposing site on high ground to the east of the town. The Misses Lawrence's school had gone up in the world. It had acquired extensive new buildings, a new (Anglican) hapel and a new name – 'Roedean'. Today, the only English girls' chool that still bears any trace of its Unitarian origin is Channing chool in Highgate, North London, founded, like Roedean, in 1885. t has Unitarian governors and offers scholarships to ministers' aughters.

Unitarians also played a prominent part in the campaign to give omen access to university education. One of their number, Elisabeth eid, founded the 'Ladies' College' (later called Bedford College) hich first gave women entrance to the University of London. The dmission of women to the ancient universities of England owed much the efforts of Barbara Leigh Smith, the principal founder of Girton ollege, Cambridge. As for medical schools, these remained closed to omen until the mid-nineteenth century. The world's first woman octor was a Unitarian, Elizabeth Blackwell, who was trained in merica and whose name was put on the British Medical Register in 859.

oday, women continue to play an important part in the Unitarian ovement. As in most other denominations, the women in the pews sually outnumber the men. They take on many of the most urdensome jobs, such as chairperson, treasurer or secretary of the ongregation. Many churches have active branches of the Women's eague, a national organisation with international contacts, and there a continuing concern for feminist issues. Many women also serve on e committees of District Associations and on the council of the eneral Assembly, the governing body of the denomination. Since the rmation of the Assembly in 1928, seven of the annually elected residents have been women.

OMEN MINISTERS   Unitarians were the first denomination in Britain accept women into their ministry. The first woman minister was the everend Gertrud von Petzold, who came originally from Germany. fter three years' training at Manchester College, Oxford, she served s minister in Leicester from 1904 to 1908 and later in Birmingham. ince she first broke the sex-barrier a total of thirty-three women have ntered the Unitarian ministry in Britain. Today there are twenty omen ministers. One of them, the Reverend Penelope Laws,

45

minister of Dean Row Chapel in Wilmslow, Cheshire, is pictured on the front cover of this book.

MARGARET BARR   One of the Unitarians' most outstanding women ministers – who became 'a legend in her own lifetime' – was Margaret Barr. A Yorkshirewoman of Methodist parentage, she joined the Cambridge Unitarian Church while a student at Girton. After training at Manchester College, Oxford, followed by a six-year pastorate at Rotherham, she decided to go to India. In 1932, hearing that a minister was needed to serve the little group of Unitarian churches in the Khasi Hills of Assam in north-east India, she wrote to the committee responsible for making the appointment: 'Here I am: send me.' However, the committee refused to allow a woman to go to 'such a lonely post'. So Margaret got herself a teaching job in Calcutta and began to pay unofficial visits to the Khasi Hills. Eventually, through sheer determination, she won: in 1936 she was given official charge of the churches there. And there she remained, apart from brief visits to Britain and America, for thirty-seven years. For more than ten years her permanent base was at Shillong, the capital of Assam, where she devoted her energies to the care of the churches and also founded two schools. By the late 1940s the schools were well-enough established to be handed over to others and she began to look around for a fresh field of service.

Margaret Barr had never forgotten what her friend Mahatma Gandhi had said to her when she first arrived in India: he had advised her to go and work in the villages 'serving those who need you most'. So she determined to leave the comfort and security of the town and settle in a remote village. She chose Kharang, a place that could be reached only after a 25-kilometre walk along a rough and stony track. Here she established her Rural Centre, with a residential school attended by children from the surrounding countryside. Kong ('Sister') Barr was not just a teacher, however: she was by turns nurse, midwife, counsellor, sustainer and friend to a great company of people. Meanwhile, she continued to act as superintendent minister of the Unitarian Union of the Khasi and Jaintia Hills – arranging services, running Sunday schools and training lay leaders in a score of scattered churches. A young Australian who spent a year helping at

46

Margaret Barr

Kharang described Margaret Barr's job as 'one of the loneliest and toughest in the world'. But she loved it. Under her care the Rural Centre flourished and became famous throughout the region. Here she lived until she died, still in harness, in 1973. She was in her seventy-fifth year.

Not long before she died, Margaret Barr spoke about the faith that had sustained her through the years. 'It grows increasingly more precious with every year that passes. It is here at Kharang in the midst of all this wild loveliness that it has flowered and fruited.'

47

Think about . . .

Find out all you can about Florence Nightingale
childhood and family background. Your local library w:
probably have a copy of C. Woodham-Smith's biograp
of her.

What part do women play in the life of the Churches
your locality? Do their functions vary from one Church
another?

What are the arguments for and against wome
becoming ministers?

An International Movement

There are Unitarians in most parts of the world – in India, Australia, Africa and America, as well as on the continent of Europe.

EUROPE   A fully organised Unitarian Church has existed in Transylvania since 1568. Its founder and first bishop was Francis David, a former Calvinist leader who had

Unitarians have groups in many countries around the world

49

The Unitarian Church of the First Congregation in Cluj-Napoca (Koloszvar) next to the Unitarian headquarters in Romania

abandoned belief in the Trinity after studying the Scriptures and conversing with some followers of an Italian heretic called Socinus. His chief supporter was the ruler of Transylvania, John Sigismund, the only Unitarian king in history and the first European ruler to grant complete religious freedom to his subjects. The young Church suffered much persecution and some of its members were forcibly reconverted to Catholicism. Today it has over 80 000 members, most of whom are in Transylvania (now part of Romania) and the rest in Hungary, around Budapest. They are governed by two bishops and three lay presidents, one of whom is the son of the composer Bartok. They have close ties with Unitarians in Britain: some of their theological students go to Britain to study at Manchester College, Oxford and the Unitarian College, Manchester.

There are a few Unitarian congregations in West Germany and Czechoslovakia, and one in Denmark. There are also various bodies which, although not Unitarian in name, are liberal in their religious outlook, such as the Remonstrant Brotherhood of Holland, the Free Christian Union of Switzerland and the 'associations libérales' within the Reformed Churches of France and Belgium. But of all these liberal Christian communities it is the Non-Subscribing Presbyterian Church of Ireland (so called because it does not 'subscribe to', i.e. agree to, any fixed creeds), with thirty-two congregations in Ulster and two in Eire, which has the closest links with Unitarians in England, Wales and Scotland. This long-established Church is affiliated to the British General Assembly and most of its ministers were trained at the Unitarian College, Manchester.

AMERICA The largest group of Unitarian Churches in the world is in the U.S.A. They originated in a reform movement within the Congregational Churches of New England in the second half of the eighteenth century. Like the English Presbyterians, many of the New England Congregationalists became discontented with the prevailing Calvinist doctrine. They were strongly influenced by John Taylor's *Scripture Doctrine of Original Sin*, copies of which had found their way across the Atlantic. Later they were influenced by the writings of Lindsey and of Priestley, who, as we have seen, himself emigrated to America in 1794. By the early 1800s many Congregationalists had

William Ellery Channing

begun to call themselves 'Unitarian'. The heartland of the movement was in Massachusetts, where most of the parish churches became Unitarian, including First Church, Plymouth, which had been founded by the Pilgrim Fathers in 1620. The biggest concentration was around Boston, where William Ellery Channing, the famous preacher and writer, was a minister. In 1825 the American Unitarian Association was founded by a group of young graduates of the nearby Harvard Divinity School, then coming under Unitarian control. It was in Boston, too, that Ralph Waldo Emerson ministered for a time before resigning his pastorate to devote his time to writing. Emerson

isliked the 'cold, hard Unitarianism' of his day and advocated a
armer, more 'spiritual' approach to religion. He urged people to
sten to 'the voice of God in their souls'. He and those who thought
ke him were called 'Transcendentalists'. They had a great influence
n the Unitarian movement, not only in America but also in Britain.
ymns of the Spirit, produced by 'the two Sams', Johnson and
ongfellow, set people singing in a new way throughout the English-
peaking world.

In the twentieth century the Unitarian movement in America has
xpanded considerably. In 1961 the denomination merged with the
Iniversalists, another group of liberal Churches with a similar
istory. Today their combined numbers are about 150 000 and they
re still growing. They have many fine new buildings; some of the
iost spectacular were designed by the famous architect Frank Lloyd
Vright, a descendant of Unitarian emigrants from the 'Black Spot' of
ardiganshire. Unitarian Universalist Churches now extend right
cross America. The old-established congregations on the eastern
eaboard are generally more Christian in outlook than the newer ones
a the middle and west of America, many of which are frankly
iumanist'; but they are united by a common commitment to the civil
ights movement. Malvina Reynolds, the well-known song-writer and
earless opponent of the Klu Klux Klan, was an active Unitarian. So
oo was James Reeb, the young Boston minister who was beaten to
eath by three white men while supporting civil rights in Selma,
Alabama in 1965. (His attackers were later acquitted by an all-white
ary.)

American Unitarian Universalists have always had close ties with
Unitarians in Britain and with the other congregations affiliated to the
British General Assembly that are found in Canada, Australia, New
Zealand and South Africa. They attend each other's Assembly
meetings, they read each other's publications, they sing each other's
hymns and they even exchange ministers. The Americans have also
given a great deal of assistance to the Unitarian Churches in India.

NDIA   The Unitarians in India were mentioned in the previous
hapter. Their churches were founded not by Europeans (Unitarians
lo not have missionaries) but by native Indians. The oldest

congregation – at Madras – was founded in 1795 by an Indian who ha
become a Unitarian while working as a domestic servant in Englan
But the main group of churches is the one in north-east India whic
was served by Margaret Barr. How they came to be there is a long an
complicated story.

In the early years of the nineteenth century lived a Hindu prince
Bengal called Ram Mohun Roy. He was a religious seeker wh
dissatisfied both with Hinduism and with the faith proclaimed b
Christian missionaries, decided that Unitarianism came closest
what he called 'genuine Christianity'. So in 1833 he came to Englan
to see Dr Lant Carpenter, minister of Lewin's Mead chapel, Bristo
While there he fell ill and died, but his influence lived on, for he ha
founded a religious reform movement called the Brahmo Samaj tha
was to play an important part in the creation of modern India. (Brist
Cathedral recently produced a booklet about Ram Mohun Roy
coincide with the 150th anniversary of his death.) After his deat
members of the movement maintained close links with Englis
Unitarians and especially with their friends in Bristol. The
entertained Mary Carpenter on her three lengthy visits to India in th
1860s and 1870s. When in England, one of them would sometime
preach in Lewin's Mead. They were also in touch with America
Unitarians, who in the 1850s sent a minister to Calcutta to help the
in their work.

One day in 1885 the American minister had a visitor, sent to him b
the local Brahmo Samaj. Hajom Kissor Singh came from the Kha
Hills of Assam and was barely out of his teens. He had been educate
by Welsh Calvinists and was one of their best Bible scholars, but, afte
long heart-searching, he had decided that the Christianity as taught b
the missionaries was not 'the true religion of Jesus'. So he left his hom
village and went to Calcutta in search of someone to help him in hi
quest. The American minister gave him books and pamphlets and
after reading them, Kissor decided that he too was a Unitarian. Tw
years later, at the age of twenty-two, he founded the first Unitaria
church in the Khasi Hills. By the time of his death in 1923 there wer
twenty churches, with a membership of 2000. Since then the numbe
of churches has increased further, under the leadership of Margare
Barr and the local people whom she trained.

ALL FAITHS   At the beginning of this century the Unitarian Churches of Britain and America founded the International Association for Religious Freedom to bring together religious liberals from all over the world. Since then its membership has expanded to include liberal groups from half a dozen European countries: the latest to join is the (Anglican) Modern Churchmen's Union. Moreover, in recent years a number of liberal religious organisations from right outside the Christian tradition have joined the Association: the largest member group is now the Rissho Kosei-Kai, a lay Buddhist movement from Japan.

This new development is generally welcomed by British Unitarians, who have long advocated a closer dialogue with other world religions. The systematic study of non-Christian religions was pioneered in this country by Lant Carpenter's grandson, Estlin Carpenter, who began to lecture on Buddhism, Hinduism and Islam in the late 1870s. Another Unitarian minister, Travers Herford, was held in great esteem by Jewish scholars for producing the first unbiased study of Judaism in the New Testament period. Unitarians

Young people of the International Association for Religious Freedom at a Youth Encounter in Calcutta, India, 1983

PEACE ON EARTH

Six children hold symbols of major world faiths: Buddhist, Unitarian, Hindu, Christian, Taoist and Jewish

were also among the first supporters of the World Congress of Faiths which organises some impressive 'all-faiths' services, often on Unitarian premises.

Perhaps the most inspiring of all the inter-faith services is the one held each September in Bristol, when the congregation of Lewin's Mead Meeting is joined by members of the Indian community from all over Britain. They come together to honour the memory of two great men, Ram Mohun Roy and his friend Lant Carpenter, who, 150 years ago, began the work of breaking down the barriers between Christianity and the other great religions of the world.

Think about . . .

'Little Boxes' and 'What have they done to the rain?' are two of Malvina Reynolds' best-known songs. Try to find copies of some of her other songs and discuss their meaning.

One of the outstanding figures in the Brahmo Samaj was Rabindranath Tagore. Read about him in an encyclopaedia and see if you can find any collections of the translations of his poems in your library.

Make a list of the non-Christian religions in your area and find out whether any inter-faiths services have been held. Why not suggest holding one in your own church or school?

9

The Future of Unitarianism

In the previous chapters much has been said about the past, and this is understandable. For Unitarians, as for all religious bodies, the past is of great importance. They feel a need to recall the achievements of their predecessors and to see themselves as the heirs of a great tradition. It matters to them, for example, that Eleanor Dixon, who was elected President of their General Assembly in 1982, is a direct descendant of four ministers ejected in 1662 and also of John Taylor and David Davis, the distinguished theologians mentioned earlier in this book. It meant a great deal to the delegates to that Assembly, meeting that year in South Wales, to make a pilgrimage to Llwynrhydowen to see the chapel where David Davis had once ministered and from which, in 1876, the Unitarians had been evicted by a landlord who disliked their radical views. They were able to stand on the spot where the Reverend Gwilym Marles had then stood, with his back to the chained gate of the chapel-yard, preaching in the open air to a crowd of 3000. An awareness of the continuity of its tradition helps to hold a denomination together and determine its identity.

But Unitarians recognise that to dwell too much on the past can be morbid. It is as depressing for them as it is for other denominations to recall just how much more numerous and influential they were 'years ago'. For a Unitarian minister in London, trying to address the world over the heads of his modest congregation, it might not be encouraging to remember that when James Martineau preached at Little Portland Street Chapel in the 1860s, his hearers often included Lord John Russell, W. E. Gladstone, George Eliot, Charles Darwin and a good many other distinguished people who had strayed in for the service. 'There were giants in those days!' is not the kind of remark that will stimulate present endeavours.

So Unitarians are determined to be 'forward-looking'. They like to see themselves as a genuine *movement* – a group of people 'on the move'. They do not like to think themselves as being 'the same yesterday, today and for ever'. Over the last two hundred years their beliefs and practices have changed more rapidly and more radically than those of any other denomination. This gives them a feeling that they are, and always will be, 'ahead of their time'.

Where then are they heading? On this, as on every other topic, Unitarians are divided. At one extreme are the 'Free Christians' who wish to remain part of the Church Universal; at the other are those who wish to move 'beyond Christianity' to a universal 'theism' (or perhaps even 'humanism') that embraces the insights of all the great world religions and philosophies. Where the average Unitarian stands it is difficult to say, but it is likely that most people, if they had to choose, would prefer to remain within the Christian fold.

The choice, of course, is not theirs alone. Although the direction that the movement takes will be largely determined by the wishes of its members, it will also be influenced by the attitudes of other denominations.One reason why some Unitarians wish to move 'beyond Christianity' is that so often in the past the Christian Church has given them the cold shoulder.

In some ways the cold-shouldering is understandable. Throughout their history Unitarians have been a disruptive influence. They have disturbed the peace of the Church and have criticised accepted beliefs and well-tried customs. They are the 'awkward squad' of Christendom, and so are perhaps better out of the way. On the other hand, some Christians are worried by what appears to be a serious shortage of people who are prepared to think for themselves. For example, the Archbishop of York, writing in *The Times* in October 1982, suggested that to promote the health of the Church of England, its members needed to show a greater independence of mind. 'We must learn to grapple with the mysteries of the faith and come to some informed conclusions about them, even at the cost of personal discomfort and confusion. Better an adventurous heretic than a numbed conformist.'

The story of the Unitarians is the story of a group of 'adventurous heretics', moving through time. It has been their lot to meet with persecution, controversy, perplexity, division. But they feel that there is an inner purpose in which they can safely trust, and, with this knowledge, they continue to travel hopefully.

Important Dates

1662	Act of Uniformity: the 'Great Ejection'.
1689	Toleration Act.
1719	Salters' Hall debate.
1740	John Taylor's *Scripture Doctrine of Original Sin*.
1757	Opening of Warrington Academy.
1774	Theophilus Lindsey opens Essex Street Chapel.
1782	Joseph Priestley's *History of the Corruptions of Christianity*.
1791	Foundation of Unitarian Society for promoting Christian Knowledge.
1794	Priestley emigrates to America.
1798	First Mechanics' Institute is opened (in Nottingham).
1806	Expulsion of Joseph Cooke from Methodist Conference.
1807	The Misses Lawrence's school opens at Gateacre.
1813	Unitarian Relief Act: Unitarian beliefs no longer illegal.
	Foundation of Scottish Unitarian Association.
1818	John Pounds founds first Ragged School (in Portsmouth).

1825	Formation of British and Foreign Unitarian Association.
1833	Death of Ram Mohun Roy in Bristol.
1835	Establishment of first Domestic Mission.
1836	James Martineau's *Rationale of Religious Enquiry*.
1854	Mary Carpenter opens girls' reformatory in Bristol.
1873–6	Joseph Chamberlain is mayor of Birmingham.
1876	Eviction of Unitarians from Llwynrhydowen Chapel.
1881	Formation of National Conference of Unitarian and Kindred Congregations.
1900	Death of James Martineau. Foundation of International Association for Religious Freedom.
1904	Gertrud von Petzold becomes first woman minister in Britain.
1928	Formation of General Assembly of Unitarian and Free Christian Churches.
1936	Margaret Barr settles in the Khasi Hills.
1962	Official celebration of tercentenary of Great Ejection: Unitarians excluded!

Further Reading

A Dream Come True by MARGARET BARR (Lindsey Press, 1974).

Finding the Place by BRUCE FINDLOW (Lindsey Press, 1974).

History of the Hibbert Trust by ALAN RUSTON (The Hibbert Trust, 1984).

Joseph Priestley – Man of Science by JOHN MCLACHLAN (Merlin Books, 1983).

A Liberal Religious Heritage by ANDREW HILL (Lindsey Press, 1984).

Living in the Questions by RALPH HELVERSON (Lindsey Press, 1977).

On Being a Unitarian by A. PHILLIP HEWETT (Canadian Unitarian Council & Lindsey Press, third edition 1977).

Unitarianism by JOHN HOSTLER (The Hibbert Trust, 1981).

William Roscoe by GRAHAM MURPHY (1981).

Songs for Living and Words of Worship (Lindsey Press, 1972).

Hymns for Living (General Assembly, 1984).

A fuller further reading list is available from the Unitarian Information Department or the Essex Hall Bookshop (see Useful Addresses).

A range of free pamphlets, etc., is also available from the Unitarian Information Department.

Useful Addresses

The Unitarian Information Department, the Unitarian Headquarters, and the Essex Hall Bookshop are all at: Essex Hall, 1-6 Essex Street, Strand, London WC2R 3HY.

Dr Williams's Library and the Hibbert Trust are both at: 14 Gordon Square, London WC1H 0AG.

Training Colleges

Manchester College, Mansfield Road, Oxford OX1 3TD. Unitarian College, Daisy Bank Road, Victoria Park, Manchester M14 5QL.